CLASSICAL ORNAMENT

OF THE EIGHTEENTH

CENTURY

CLASSICAL ORNAMENT

OF THE EIGHTEENTH CENTURY

Designed & engraved by Michelangelo Pergolesi

with an introduction by EDWARD A. MASER

Professor of Art, the University of Chicago

DOVER PUBLICATIONS, INC., NEW YORK

Published in Canada by General Publishing Company, Ltd.,
30 Lesmill Road, Don Mills, Toronto, Ontario.
Published in the United Kingdom by Constable and Company, Ltd.,
10 Orange Street, London WC 2.

Classical Ornament of the Eighteenth Century is an unabridged republication of an untitled and undated volume of ornamental sheets designed, engraved and published in London by Michelangelo Pergolesi between 1777 and 1792 (each plate was dated). A new introduction has been written specially for this volume by Edward A. Maser.

Standard Book Number: 486-22389-2

Library of Congress Catalog Card Number: 75-82792

Manufactured in the United States of America

DOVER PUBLICATIONS, INC.
180 Varick Street, New York, N. Y. 10014

Introduction to the Dover Edition

IN 1758, when the brilliant young Scottish archi-tect Robert Adam returned home to England from Rome after a four-year stay in Italy, he carried with him countless drawings of classical antiquities he had made during those years. They were soon to be the source for the decorative style he developed and which eventually bore his name. In Italy he left a world fer-menting with new ideas and filled with what were to become great names in the history of art and taste. Rome was where Johann Joachim Winckelmann was preaching a new aesthetic, rejecting the centuries-old traditions of the Renaissance and the Baroque, and urging an emulation of the "noble simplicity and quiet grandeur" of ancient Greek and Roman art. There great artists like Anton Raphael Mengs were trying to put Winckelmann's ideas into practice, producing paintings which seemed to be a complete departure from the past and to herald a new kind of art, one combining all the ideal beauty of the ancient world with the new moral and philosophical ideas of the second half of the eight-eenth century, the period commonly known as the Enlightenment.

The city of Rome itself did much to engender these new tastes and ideas, not the Baroque city of Bernini and Borromini, but the ancient one of Trajan and Hadrian. Giovanni Battista Piranesi was gaining fame with his etchings of views of the city, evoking images of its past glories and its magnificence, images still very much valid, or at least appreciated, today. Following a tradition going back to the Renaissance, when Raphael

had been head of all archeological excavations and researches in Rome, Piranesi also engaged in the serious study of the monuments of Roman art, measuring, drawing, and eventually publishing the results of his antiquarian researches. His work on the Dalmatian coast, at Pola, was perhaps the most important example of this sort of activity on his part outside of Rome. Fol-lowing Piranesi's example, Robert Adam had also gone to the eastern shore of the Adriatic to make his most important studies. He went to Spalato, the present-day Split, to make careful studies of the huge palace built there by Emperor Diocletian in the early fourth cen-tury A.D.

Equally important for his future plans as an architect and designer were the many highly skilled and talented artists, primarily in the graphic arts, whom Robert Adam had met in Italy. Many were eager to collaborate with him, and some could even be lured into accom-panying or following him to England. He eventually worked with several of them after his return to London. Some, like Giovanni Battista Ciprani, had preceded him there in 1755; others, like Francesco Bartolozzi, followed him in 1764. They must all have known each other at some time in Rome, for Bartolozzi and Cipriani, both Florentines, had also worked and studied there. Michelangelo Pergolesi, whom Adam specifically called to London to work with him on the publications he was preparing, undoubtedly also belonged to this group in Rome.

Robert Adam's chief publication, the result of his

[v]

antiquarian studies in Dalmatia, was entitled *Ruins of the Palace of the Emperor Diocletian at Spalatro* (sic) *in Dalmatia* and appeared in London in 1764. With it he introduced fashionable and scholarly London to the results of his long studies, and to the ornament he had found on this great monument of late Imperial Roman art. It became a type of ornament much favored in his day, and made him famous. It is still known today as "Adam ornament."

Like Winckelmann, who based his epoch-making history of ancient art and his fervid appreciation of Greek art on Roman copies of earlier sculpture; and like Piranesi, who based his own glorification of Roman art on, among other things, pre-Roman Greek and Etruscan monuments, Adam, thinking he was replacing the current Rococo ornament of his day with the pure and classic ornament of the ancients, had really found in the palace of Diocletian a very "baroque" example of Roman architecture. Yet it was a light and graceful ornament which Adam presented. Its combination of finely drawn architectural, figural, and vegetable motifs was elegantly spread across a surface with restraint and with a very formal symmetry. It had little to do with the forceful and often too luxuriant decoration of earlier Roman art. It was undoubtedly viewed so favorably by the public just because it was anything but a radical departure from the taste of the recent past. Adam based all his later designing on these studies, and their influence is clearly to be seen in all his work as designer and decorator.

Cipriani, Bartolozzi, and Pergolesi, it seems, settled down in London permanently (Cipriani, and presumably Pergolesi, died there, while Bartolozzi moved to Portugal in 1802, where he remained until his death in 1815). They became esteemed and active members of London's artistic community, producing the graceful and charming stipple engravings, mezzotints, calling cards, and ornament prints which are still considered among the finest productions of their kind made during the period in England. While Bartolozzi and Cipriani went on to become famous in their own right and had well-documented careers, Pergolesi remained forever

somewhat in the background, and almost nothing is known of his life and career, not even the dates when he was born and when he died. Aside from his work for Adam, he produced one publication in his own name, which remains his monument, his series of prints, *Designs for various ornaments, etc.*, published over a long period, from 1777 to 1801.* These prints first appeared as loose sheets, without letterpress of any kind, and offered, as has been said "a perfect treasurehouse of fine Italian designs." In them, Pergolesi presented designs for almost every conceivable kind of decoration—panel and pilaster ornament, trophies, friezes, cornices, doors, ceilings, urns, balustrades, ironwork, plasterwork, and even chairs and settees. The ornament consisted largely of plant forms, architectural moldings, and figures, combined in most cases to make so-called "grotesque" ornament, itself of ancient Roman origin, but popular in Europe since the Renaissance, when it was rediscovered. Many of the designs of delicate tracery suggest the finest filigree, while others clearly show their debt to Raphael, and not to the anonymous masters of the palace workshops in Spalato. Pergolesi particularly favored using a panel or medallion within his interlaced all-over design, in the center of the ornamental field. He would depict some bit of idyllic or mythological subject matter within these medallions, often making them look like cameos. Cipriani, Bartolozzi, Angelica Kauffmann, and others were specialists in painting and engraving these little scenes, usually including amorini, some genre subject, or some motif derived from ancient relief sculpture. In his print series, Pergolesi invented and engraved all of the ornament himself, but very often the figural panels and medallions are signed by either Bartolozzi or Cipriani, who had become famous in England for these sometimes saccharine, but always graceful, little pictures.

Like Adam, Pergolesi was actually producing a sort of Rococo ornament in classical disguise. The charming prettiness of much of the figurative work, the delicacy

---

* The edition reproduced here bore no title and included sheets from 1777 to 1792.

of drawing and execution, the truly fine proportions of his designs, all find their counterpart and their origin in the beautiful Rococo ornament they were supposed to supersede. Only, together with the great dependence on archeological elements, a new emphasis on symmetry and a certain sparse restraint were substituted for the opposite qualities so prevalent earlier. The same can actually be said for all the other types of ornament popular in England and on the continent at this time. The *chinoiseries, turqueries,* and even "Gothick" designs were also, so to speak, traveling under false pretenses. They, too, were little more than the traditional basic designs, as far as formal considerations were concerned, masquerading as Oriental, Moorish, or medieval decoration. The basic structure of the ornament, its relation to the forms it was intended to embellish, and the pictorial treatment of the exotic subject matter all betrayed the survival of the age-old ornamental ideas of the Renaissance and the Baroque. This was, of course, to be expected. As much as fashions seem to change overnight, style change itself is usually a slow and almost imperceptible process, sometimes requiring a generation before it becomes evident.

Pergolesi's designs, then, represent that happy in-between period when the Rococo was being rejected in theory, but was fortunately still very much alive in spirit, and before the new emphasis on classical art became so strong, and so archeologically oriented, that it stifled the free play of the designer's imagination, or submitted it to an inflexible dogma of taste, within which there was little opportunity for originality. Nowhere in the repertory of ancient art will one find the exact counterparts of Pergolesi's or Adam's inventions, let alone their application, so that their designs cannot be called imitations. They derived the patterns from classical prototypes, but their use of these models was still a very uninhibited and imaginative one, and, happily, of great influence. The entire field of interior and furniture design of the period of George III and the early Regency in England, as well as that of the Louis XVI period in France, owed its lightness and elegance of line and its simplification of form to such designs as these. The work of Hepplewhite and Sheraton also owes much to them, and thus so does much of American furniture and decoration of the Revolutionary period. Nevertheless Pergolesi's ornament was a first step along the way toward the triumph of Neo-classicism, which found its fullest expression in the early nineteenth century.

1969   EDWARD A. MASER

SOME REFERENCE WORKS

ADAM, ROBERT. *Ruins of the Palace of the Emperor Diocletian at Spalatro in Dalmatia.* London, 1764.

CLOUSTON, K. WARREN. *The Chippendale Period in English Furniture.* London, 1897.

EVANS, JOAN. *Pattern.* Oxford, 1931.

FLEMING, JOHN. *Robert Adam and his Circle.* London, 1962.

IRWIN, DAVID. *English Neoclassical Art.* London, 1966.

JESSEN, PETER. *Der Ornamentstich.* Berlin, 1920.

Katalog der Ornamentstichsammlung der Staatlichen Kunstbibliothek Berlin. Berlin, 1936.

THIEME-BECKER, *Allgemeines Lexikon, etc.* XXVI, pp. 412–13 (Lotte Pulvermacher).

TUER, ANDREW W. *Bartolozzi and His Works.* London, 1882.

PLATES

In order to reproduce as many designs as possible in the original size, some of the 67 plates of the first edition (they are numbered 1 through 66, but there are two with the number 56) have been divided between two pages (but always facing pages) in this edition, and the order of plates has been slightly shifted in three places. It will be noted that the order of the 435 individual design numbers (the numbers 327, 343, 398, 399 and 400 do not appear) often leaps about capriciously, as in the original edition. No design has been omitted. The original edition has no prefatory matter of any kind.

1

3

Plate 1

2

Plate 1

Plate 2

4

5

6

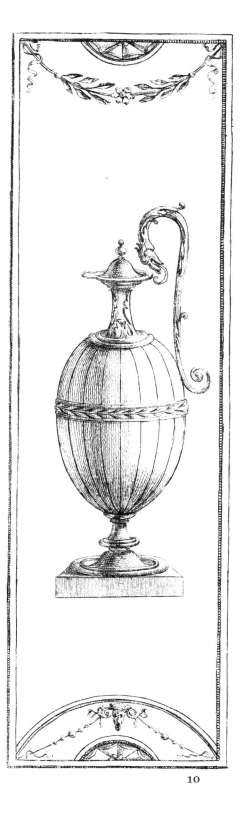

10

11

12

Plate 3

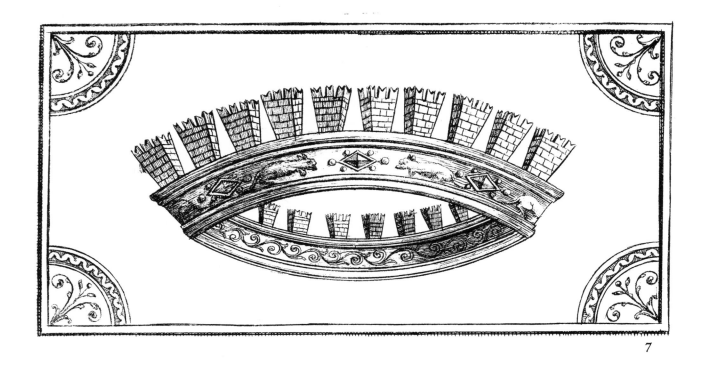

7

9

Plate 4

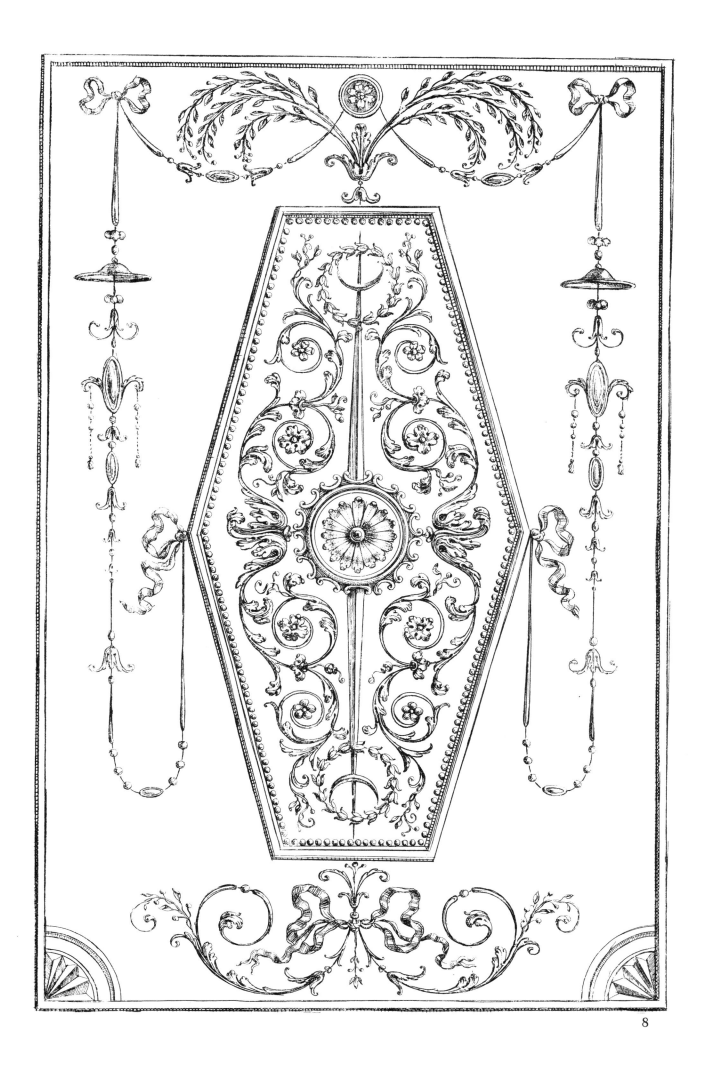

8

Plate 4

13

15

Plate 5

14

Plate 5

16

18

Plate 6

17

Plate 6

23

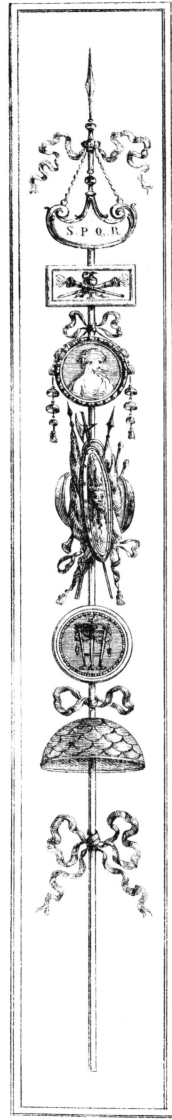

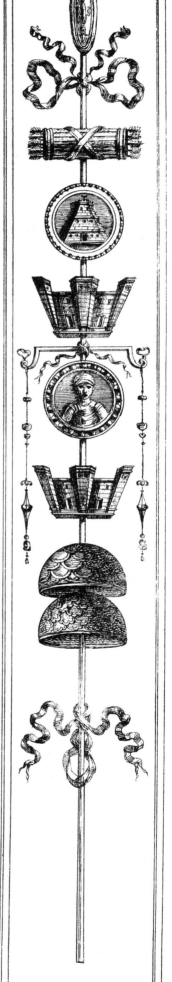

24

Plate 7

26

25

22

27

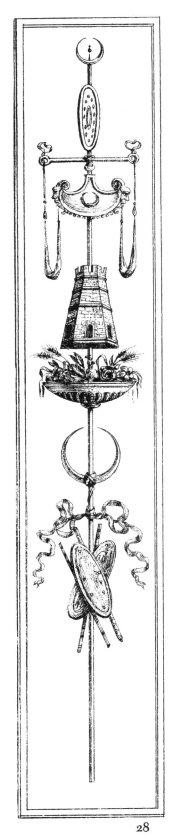

28

29

30

31

32

33

Plate 8

19

21

Plate 9

20

Plate 9

100

102

Plate 10

101

Plate 10

50

51

52

53

Plate 11

54

37

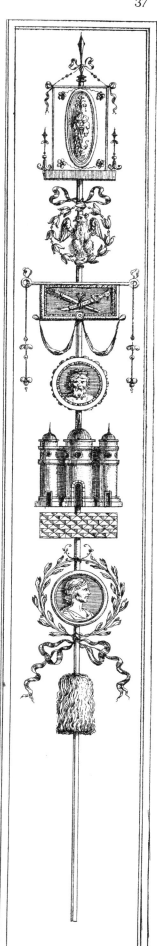

38

39

41

40

Plate 12

47

49

Plate 13

Plate 13

42

46

Plate 14

Plate 14 ⇨

43

44

45

34

36

Plate 15

35

Plate 15

55

57

Plate 16

56

Plate 16

82

83

84

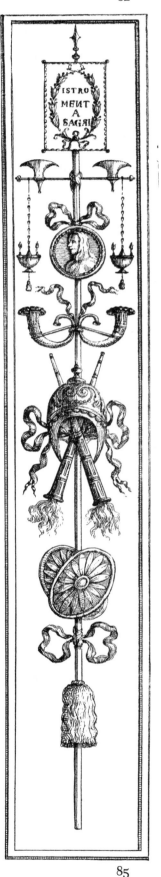

85

Plate 17

86

58

59

60

61

62

63

64

Plate 18

65

66

67

71

72

73

Plate 19

Plate 19 ⟩

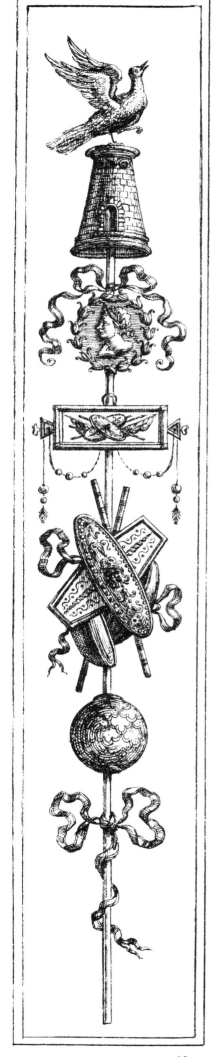

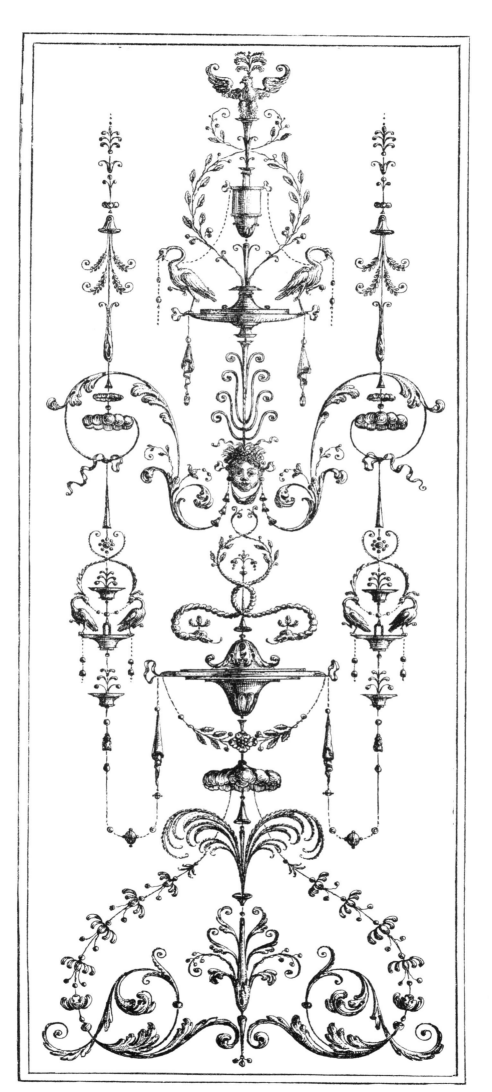

68

69

70

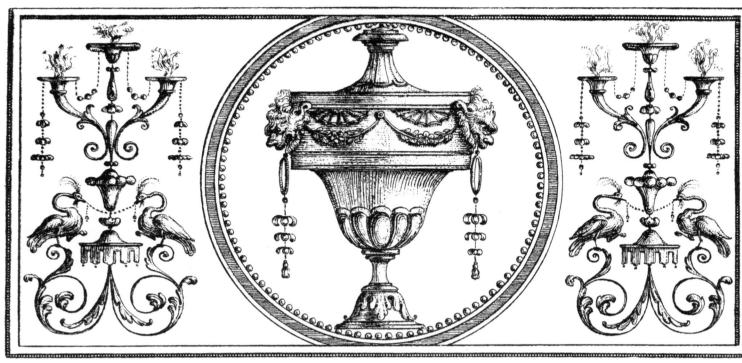

79

81

Plate 20

C.B. Cipriani del.

F. Bartolozzi Sculp.

80

Plate 20

87

89

Plate 21

88

Plate 21

104

103

99

98

104

98

96

97

98

Scale of 4 feet

Plate 22

105

106

107

Plate 23

114

113

112

110

111

109 108 109

Scale [_____] of Feet

Plate 24

74

75 76 77

78

Plate 25

90

91

92

115

116

117

Plate 26

Plate 26 ⇨

93

94

95

Plate 27

121

121

122

122

Scale of Feet

Plate 27

125

126

127

131

132

133

Plate 28

Plate 28 ⇨

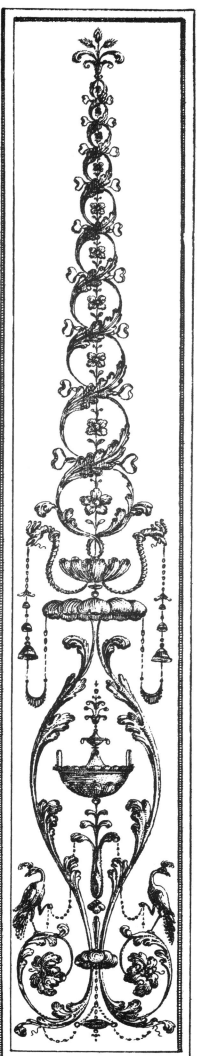

128

129

130

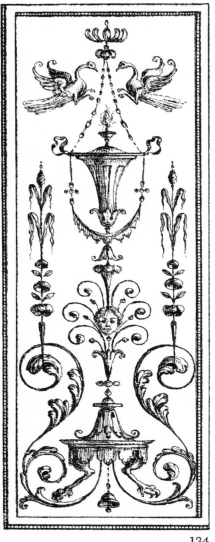

134

135

136

Plate 29

137

138

139

140

Plate 29

141   142 143

145   146 147

Plate 30

Plate 30

148

149

150

Plate 31

155

154

153

153

152

151

[51]

Scale of 4 Feet.

Plate 32

156

157

158

159

160

161

162

163

Plate 33

164

165

166

167

168

169

170

171

172

173

174

175

Plate 33

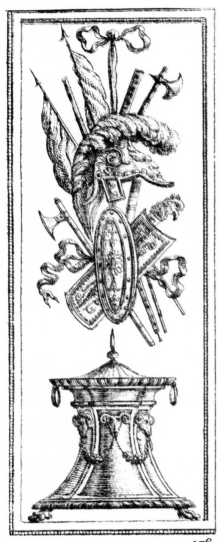

176

177

178

Plate 34

179

180

181

182

Plate 34

183

185

Plate 35

184

Plate 35

186

187

188

190

191

192

Plate 36

189

Plate 36

193

194

196

197

195

198

Plate 37

199

202   201   202

206   206

203   203

207

200

208   204   205

Scale of 4 feet

Plate 38

209

210

211

215

216

217

Plate 39

212

213

214

Plate 39

218

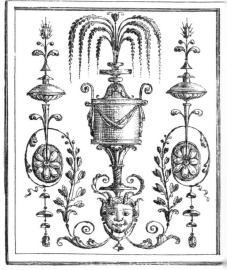

220

221

222

Plate 40

G.B. Cipriani Inv.t

F. Bartolozzi Sculp.t

Plate 40

223

227

Plate 41

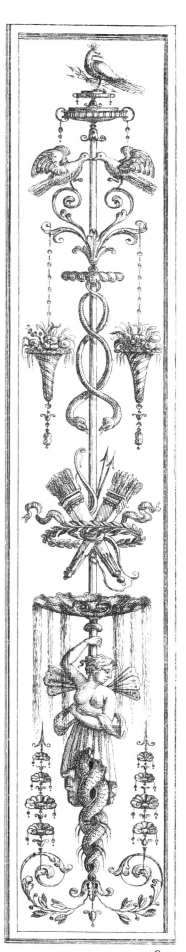

224   225   226

Plate 41

239
237
238
236
236
229
230
235
234
231
232
228
234
233
235
229
230
235

Plate 42

250

249

252

251

247

248

248

254

253

Plate 44

240

241

242

Plate 43

243

244

245

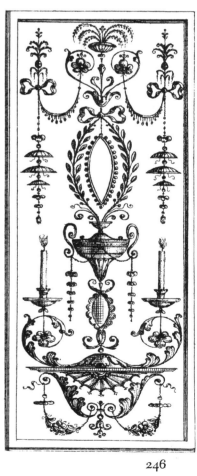

246

Plate 43

255

257

Plate 45

256

Plate 45

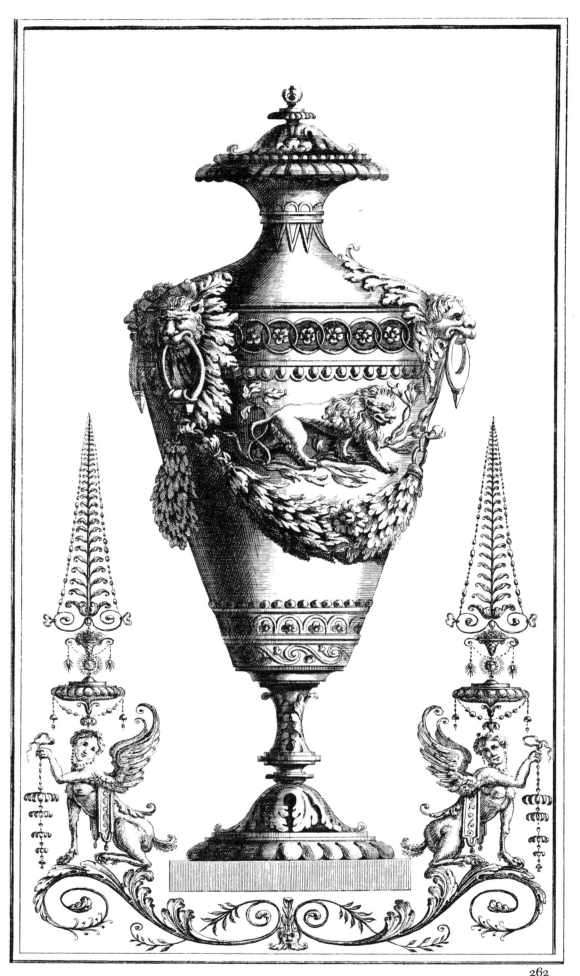

261

262

26

Plate 46

258   259   260

264   265   266

Plate 46

267

268

272

273

271

270

270

269

Plate 47

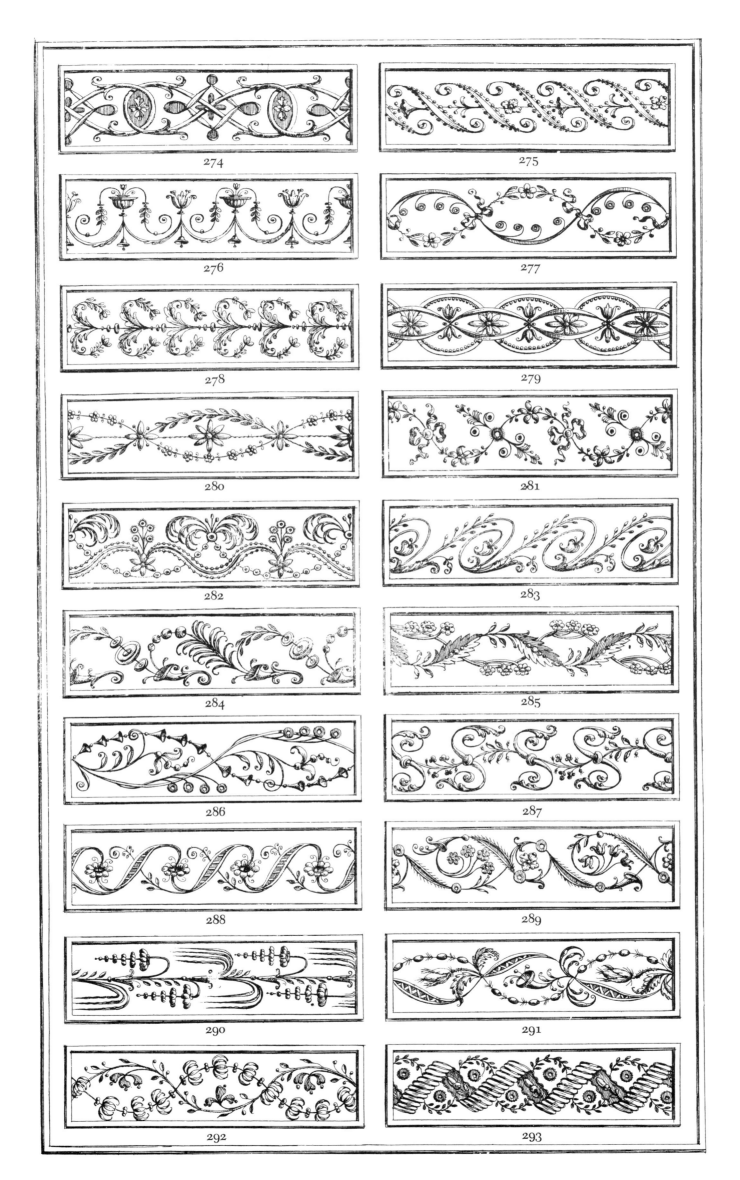

274

275

276

277

278

279

280

281

282

283

284

285

286

287

288

289

290

291

292

293

Plate 48

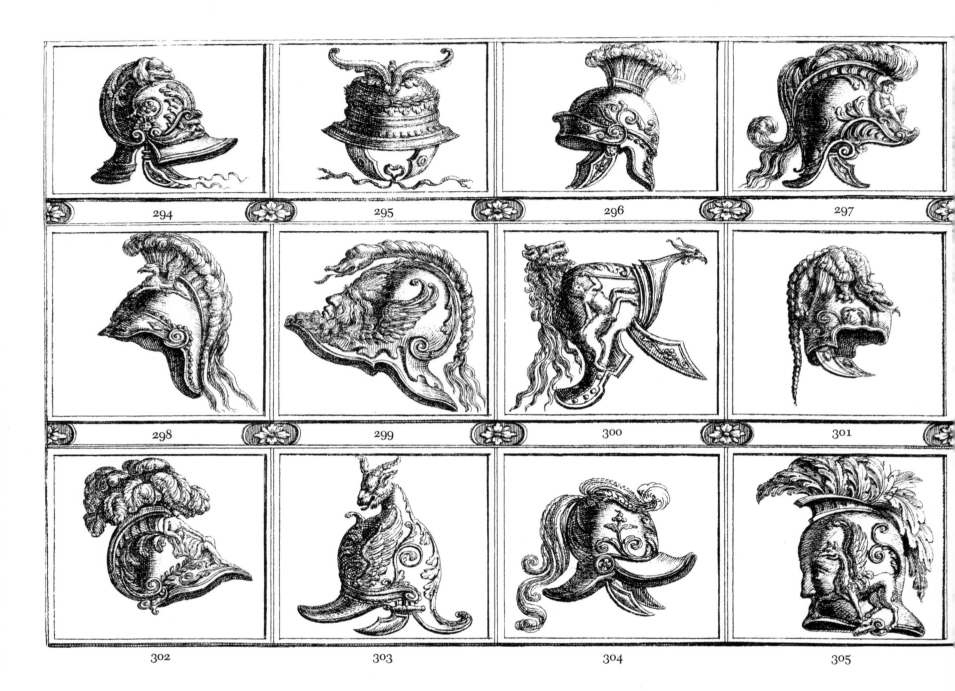

294   295   296   297

298   299   300   301

302   303   304   305

Plate 49

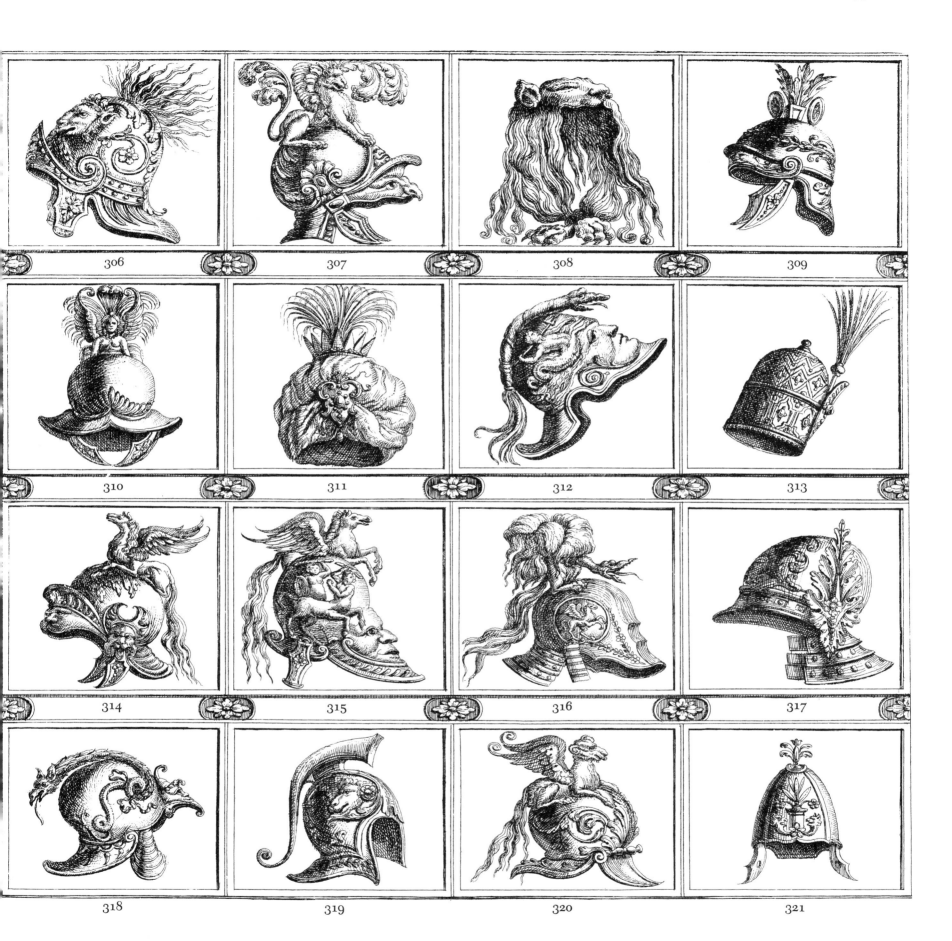

306   307   308   309

310   311   312   313

314   315   316   317

318   319   320   321

Plate 49

322

323

324

Plate 50

325

326

[80]

Plate 5

Plate 52

351

[83]

352   353   354

355   356   357

Plate 5.

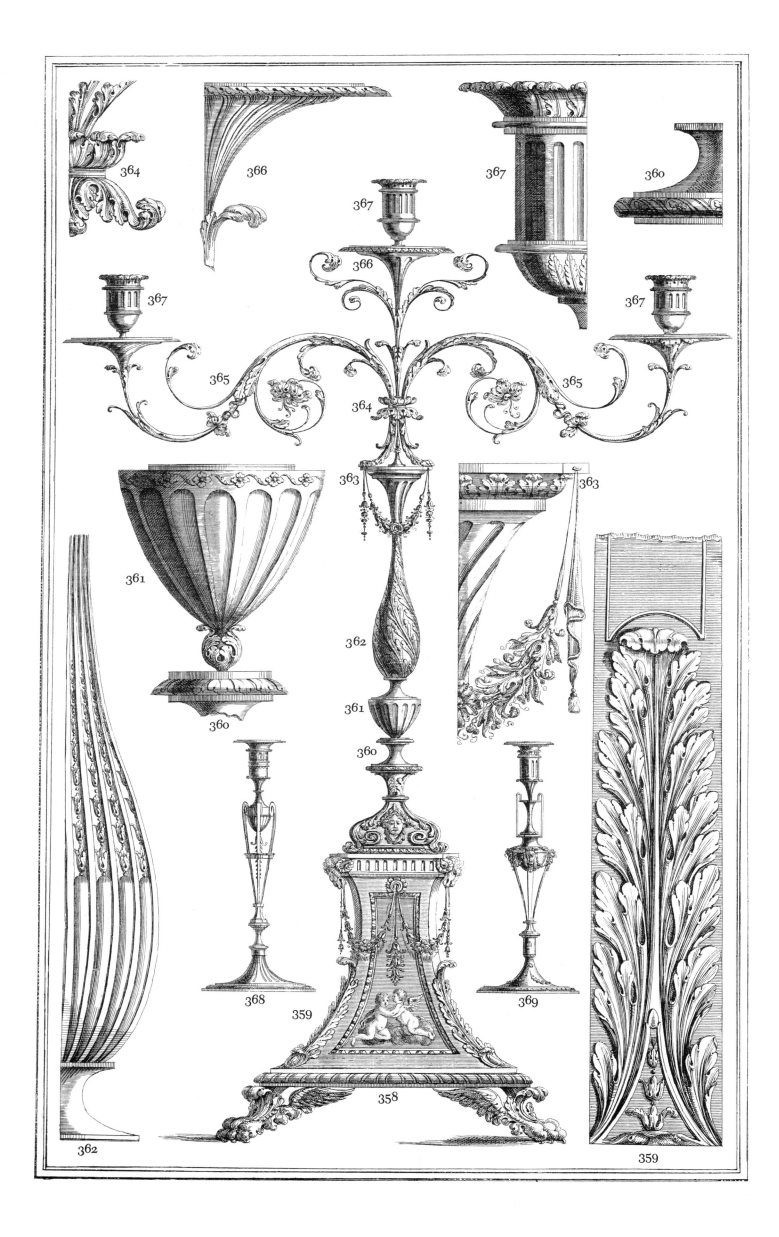

364

366

367

360

367

366

367

367

365

365

364

363

361

363

362

360

363

368

361

369

360

359

358

362

Plate 54

359

Plate 55

Plate 56 a

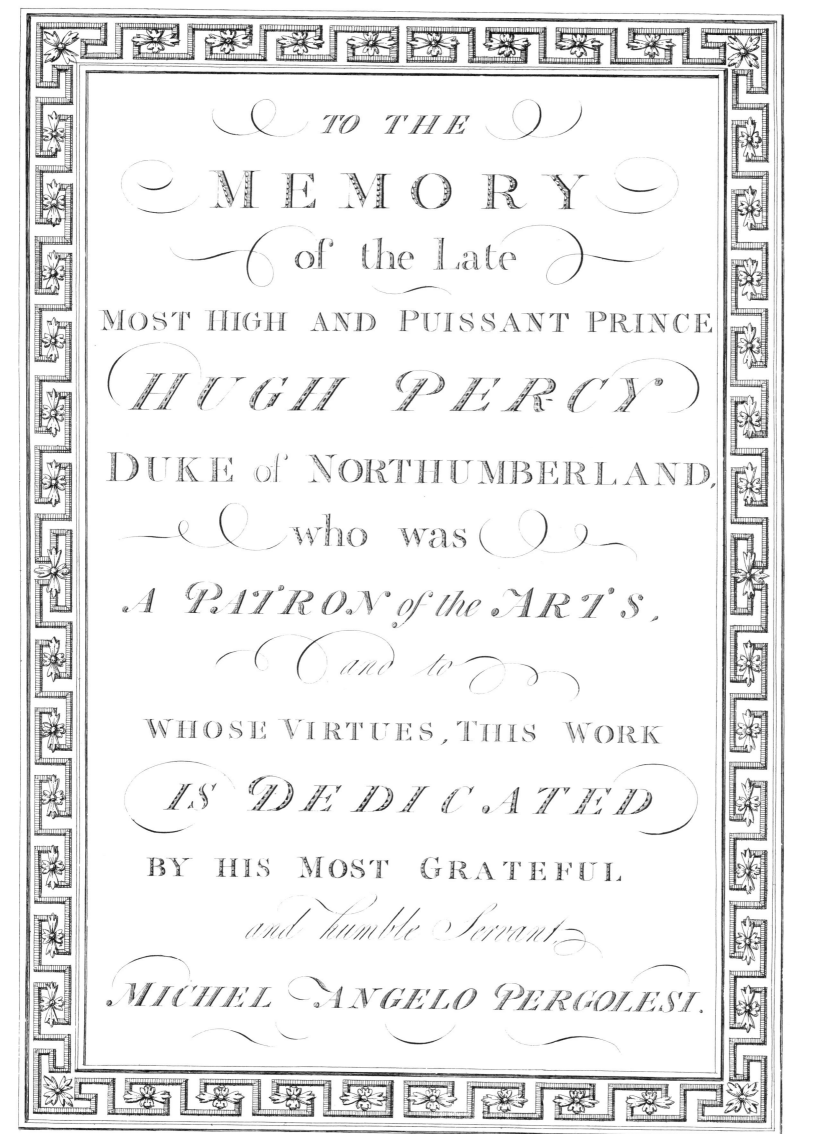

TO THE

MEMORY

of the Late

MOST HIGH AND PUISSANT PRINCE

HUGH PERCY

DUKE of NORTHUMBERLAND,

who was

A PATRON of the ARTS,

and to

WHOSE VIRTUES, THIS WORK

IS DEDICATED

BY HIS MOST GRATEFUL

and humble Servant

MICHEL ANGELO PERGOLESI.

Plate 56 b

Plate 57

393

392

394

391

390

387   388   389

386   385   386

Plate 59

373

374

375

376

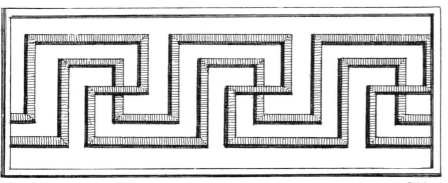

377

378

Plate 58

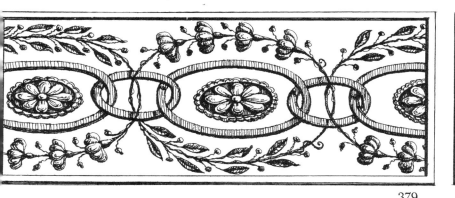

379

380

381

382

383

384

Plate 58

Plate 60

397

396

395

401

402

403

404

405

406

407

408

[93]

Plate 6

Plate 62

Plate 63

411

413 414 415 412

416 417 418

419 420

Plate 64 421 423

422 424

434

432

TO HER GRACE ELIZABETH DUCHESS OF BUCCLEUGH,

Encourager of the Artists,

Nº 13 of this Work.

Is most humbly Dedicated by

Her Graces

most obedient & obliged humble Servt.

Michael Angelo   Pergolesi

435

Plate 6

427

426

425

Plate 65

428

431

430

429

Plate 65